SUPER
SOCIAL STUDIES
INFOGRAPHICS

WORLD GEOGRAPHY THROUGH INFOGRAPHICS

Karen Latchana Kenney

graphics by
Steven Stankiewicz

Lerner Publications Company
Minneapolis

Lerner Publications Company
A division of Lerner Publishing Group, Inc.
241 First Avenue North
Minneapolis, MN 55401 USA

For reading levels and more information, look up this title at
www.lernerbooks.com.

Main text set in Univers LT Std 12/15.
Typeface provided by Adobe Systems.

Library of Congress Cataloging-in-Publication Data

Kenney, Karen Latchana.
      World geography through infographics / by Karen Latchana
   Kenney ; illustrated by Steven Stankiewicz.
         pages   cm. — (Super social studies infographics)
      Includes index.
      ISBN 978–1–4677–3461–5 (lib. bdg. : alk. paper)
      ISBN 978–1–4677–4750–9 (eBook)
      1. Geography—Audio-visual aids. 2. Communication in
   geography—Graphic methods. 3. Information visualization.
   4. Visual communication. I. Title.
   G76.K46 2015
   910—dc23   2013044300

Manufactured in the United States of America
1 – PC – 7/15/14

CONTENTS

AROUND THE WORLD

Ready to see if you'd make a good geographer? Take this quiz.

1. Do you wonder where people live in the world?

2. Have you asked why so many towns sit along rivers?

3. Do you think about how hotter temperatures affect polar bears?

4. Ever consider the effects of earthquakes?

Did you answer yes to any of those questions?

CONGRATULATIONS!

You've got the makings of a world geographer. Uncover the secrets of the world's land, waters, and countries. Learn about the wonders of the rain forest and the dangers of the Arctic. Find out how our planet's geography is constantly surprising us.

Geography isn't just about maps—though maps certainly come in handy. Geographers also use charts, graphs, and other infographics to make sense of geographical details. You can use these tools too! Let's take a trip around the world to find out how.

SMALL CAPITALS, BIG CITIES

Important things happen in a country's capital. That's the city where laws are made and government leaders manage the country. But capitals are not always the biggest and most well-known cities in a country. In fact, some capital cities are very small. Here's a look at the populations of some cities that are much bigger than their national capitals:

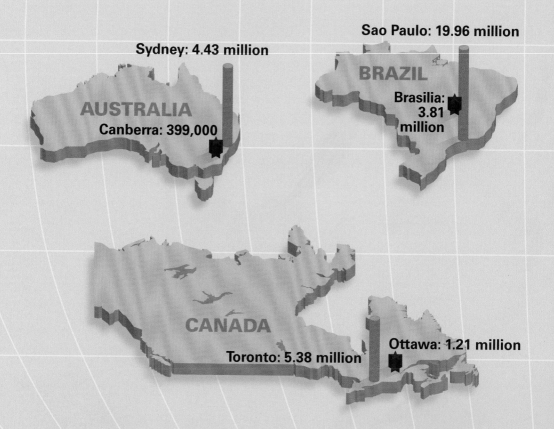

Sydney: 4.43 million

AUSTRALIA

Canberra: 399,000

Sao Paulo: 19.96 million

BRAZIL

Brasilia: 3.81 million

CANADA

Toronto: 5.38 million

Ottawa: 1.21 million

Population estimates based on most recent available data, 2009–2013

Beijing: 15.59 million

CHINA

Shanghai: 16.58 million

Quito: 1.62 million

ECUADOR

Guayaquil: 2.63 million

Astana: 800,656

KAZAKHSTAN

Almaty: 1.38 million

Casablanca: 3.25 million

Rabat: 1.77 million

MOROCCO

Pretoria: 1.40 million

Johannesburg: 3.61 million

SOUTH AFRICA

New York City: 8.34 million

UNITED STATES

Washington, DC: 4.42 million

Hanoi: 2.67 million

VIETNAM

Ho Chi Minh City: 5.98 million

capital city and its surrounding area

larger city and its surrounding area

ALL TOGETHER

People tend to group together in certain places. You won't find too many people living in the harsh environments near Earth's poles. On the other hand, the temperate zones are prime real estate thanks to their less extreme climate.

Areas with larger populations usually have plenty of natural resources close by. Water, food, and building materials are easy to find. Of course, that doesn't mean everyone has access to those resources. Some of the world's most crowded countries are home to the world's poorest people.

Take a look at the populations of countries around the world. See which ones have the most people—compared to which ones have the most wealth.

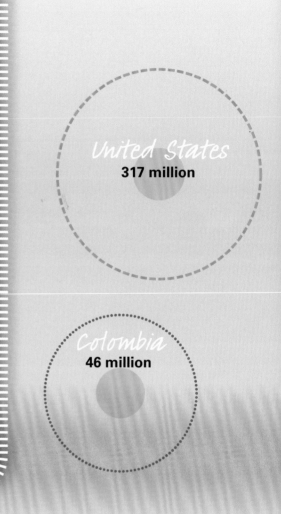

United States
317 million

Colombia
46 million

Bolivia
10.5 million

Wealth levels per adult for 2013
below $5,000
$5,000–$25,000
$25,000–$100,000
over $100,000

estimated population numbers for 2012–2013

Ireland
5 million

Russia
143 million

Iran
80 million

Kosovo
2 million

China
1.3 billion

India
1.2 billion

Rwanda
12 million

Fiji
900,000

South Africa
49 million

ON THE NILE

Look on any map and you'll see that a river and a town make the perfect pair. Rivers provide people with all kinds of useful things—from fresh, flowing water to food to a method of transportation. Many civilizations have grown along the banks of rivers. People have used the water to farm the land. They've caught fish and eaten the plants growing along the banks. They've also used the river to travel to other areas, starting new villages and towns along the way. Travel through time to glimpse some of the ancient cities that grew along the longest river in the world—the Nile River, which runs through northeastern Africa.

2925 BCE:
Memphis was founded. It became the capital of ancient Egypt.

2450–2050 BCE:
Kerma formed south of Egypt along the Nile. This advanced society made pottery and buried rulers in large tombs.

ca. 2.6 million– 248,000 BCE:
In the early Stone Age, ancient peoples lived along the river. They made pebble tools that have been found in settlements from Sudan to Egypt.

This map shows the Nile River's path through Africa. Many towns at the Nile's banks have survived thousands of years.

Alexandria
al-Fayyum •Memphis
Waset•

•Kerma
•Meroe

2040 BCE:
The city of Waset (or Thebes) grew. It replaced Memphis as the capital of ancient Egypt. Its tombs, statues, and buildings are some of the greatest of the ancient world.

1938 BCE–1756 BCE:
The city later known as al-Fayyum sat near the west bank of the Nile.

656 BCE:
Meroe was founded along the east bank of the Nile. It became the capital of Nubia.

332 BCE:
Alexandria was founded in the Nile River valley and on the Mediterranean Sea. Alexandria became Egypt's new capital and a center for learning and science.

FOOD MILES

When it's mealtime, you know where you want your food to go—your stomach. But have you thought about where it came from? Sure, the foods you love can always be found at the store. But many of those foods aren't made or grown nearby—at least not year-round. Some foods travel thousands of miles to reach grocery stores and markets around the world. Follow the journey of two shipments of oranges to a store in Australia. One orange shipment comes from a local farm. The other comes all the way from California.

ORANGE SHIPMENT NO. 1

Farm in California: Oranges are grown and harvested.

CALIFORNIA

Los Angeles International Airport: An airplane flies the oranges to Australia.

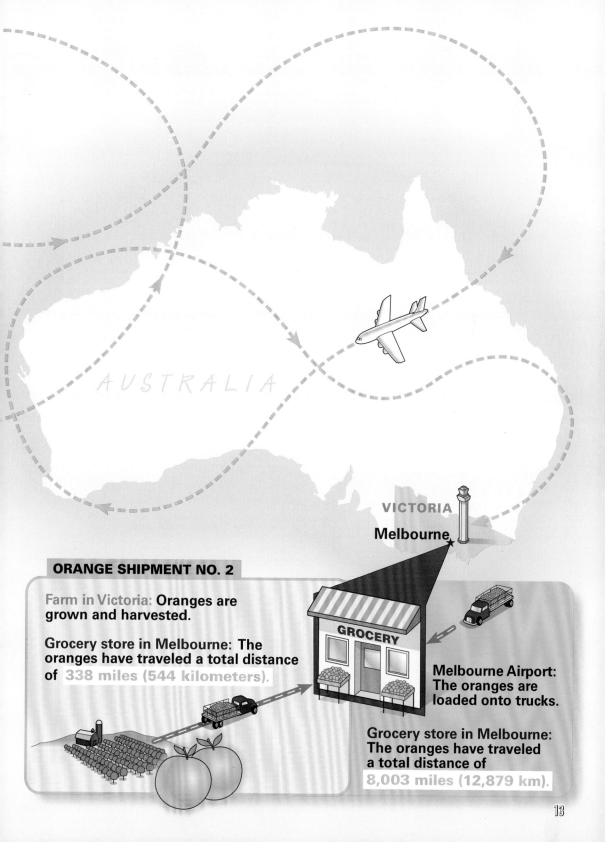

AUSTRALIA

VICTORIA

Melbourne

ORANGE SHIPMENT NO. 2

Farm in Victoria: Oranges are grown and harvested.

Grocery store in Melbourne: The oranges have traveled a total distance of **338 miles (544 kilometers).**

Melbourne Airport: The oranges are loaded onto trucks.

Grocery store in Melbourne: The oranges have traveled a total distance of **8,003 miles (12,879 km).**

THE COD WARS

When you think of borders, you probably picture dark lines that separate countries on a map. But some borders are harder to define than others. People and governments often disagree about where one nation's territory ends and another's begins.

For the remote country of Iceland, the trouble started with fish. Fish such as cod are among Iceland's most precious natural resources. So Iceland was very protective of its maritime borders. Maritime borders extend from a country's coast into the surrounding ocean. Iceland's maritime borders were at the heart of a fishing dispute between Iceland and the United Kingdom. See how Iceland's ocean territory changed during the Cod Wars.

1944: Iceland changes its maritime border agreement with the United Kingdom. The border expands from 3 to 4 miles (6 km) off Iceland's coast. The United Kingdom then bans Iceland from fishing in its waters.

1956: A European council forces the United Kingdom to obey Iceland's new border.

3 miles
(4 km)

4 miles
(6 km)

ICELAND

1958: Iceland changes its maritime border to 12 miles (19 km) off the coast.

1958–1961: The United Kingdom ignores Iceland's new border and continues to fish its waters. Iceland fights back by ramming the United Kingdom's fishing boats. This is the first Cod War.

1961: After a United Nations conference, the United Kingdom agrees to respect Iceland's 12-mile border.

12 miles (19 km)

50 miles (80 km)

1972: Iceland changes its maritime border again to extend it 50 miles (80 km) from the coast.

1972–1973: British and German ships continue fishing within Iceland's new borders. Icelandic ships cut the fishing nets of these ships.

1973: The United Kingdom and Iceland agree to allow some UK fishing within the 50-mile border for the next two years. After that, the United Kingdom must stay out of Iceland's waters.

200 miles (321 km)

1975: Iceland changes its maritime borders to a 200-mile (321 km) limit. The United Kingdom ignores the border, sparking the third Cod War.

1976: The United Kingdom agrees to respect Iceland's maritime borders. This closes off Iceland's waters to British fishing.

SEVEN SUMMITS

What are the greatest wonders of the world? That depends on whom you ask. But there's no question that our planet is full of unique landforms. Each continent boasts impressive geographic features, from plains and plateaus to hills and canyons.

The seven summits are among these natural wonders. They are the tallest mountains on each of the seven continents. Many brave explorers have tried to climb their massive heights. Here's how high these mountains reach above sea level:

ASIA

MOUNT ELBRUS
18,510 feet (5,642 m)
and 18,356 feet (5,595 m)

EUROPE

MOUNT EVEREST
29,035 feet
(8,850 m)

AFRICA

CARSTENSZ PYRAMID
(OR PUNCAK JAYA)
16,024 feet (4,884 m)

KILIMANJARO
19,340 feet
(5,895 meters)

AUSTRALIA

WORLD'S LARGEST RELIEF

Some mountains, especially volcanoes, start far below sea level. They can be measured from a base on the ocean floor to the peak. This is a mountain's total relief. Take a look at the world's largest relief—Mauna Kea, found on the island of Hawaii.

MOUNT MCKINLEY
20,320 feet (6,194 m)

NORTH
AMERICA

above sea level: 13,796 feet (4,205 m)

total height: 33,480 feet (10,205 m)

below sea level: 19, 684 feet (6,000 m)

SOUTH
AMERICA

MOUNT ACONCAGUA
22,831 feet (6,959 m)

VINSON MASSIF
16,050 feet
(4,892 m)

ANTARCTICA

TIDAL POWER

We live in an electric world. We need power for most things we do, from surfing the Internet to listening to music. Electricity can come from many different sources—fossil fuels, wind, sunlight, and even tidal waves. The world is filled with natural resources that can produce electricity. Some natural resources are renewable, such as the ocean's waves. But others are limited, such as coal, oil, and other fossil fuels.

Tidal waves, caused by gravity between Earth and the moon, contain a lot of energy. In the right locations and with the right technology, this energy can be turned into electricity. In Northern Ireland, Strangford Lough—the largest sea inlet in the United Kingdom—is a prime location for harnessing tidal power. Here's how its tidal turbine works:

SHALLOW WATER: The waters of Strangford Lough are only about 80 feet (24 m) deep in places. Shallow water produces the most energy. It also allows ships to steer easily around the turbine.

MARINE LIFE: Sea animals can avoid the slow-moving blades. Strangford Lough is home to more than 2,000 marine animal and plant species. The turbine has no known negative effects on them.

distance from shore: 1,300 feet (400m)

width of turbine: 141 feet (43 m)

sea level

seabed

TURBINE BLADES: As the current moves toward the turbine, the turbine blades move slowly. The turning blades move a generator, which makes electricity.

CURRENT: Strangford Lough has one of the world's fastest and strongest tidal currents. Waves move at an average of more than 8 feet (2.5 m) per second.

TRANSMISSION LINE: Electricity made by the turbine travels through an underwater cable to an onshore power grid. The turbine produces 1.2 megawatts of electricity per day, enough to power around 1,500 homes.

MELTING ICE

Each of Earth's climate zones has its own routine. For the polar zones, that routine involves cold, dark winters and almost equally cold, sunny summers in treeless, icy regions. For the temperate zones, it's a year of mild temperatures that help life flourish in forests and plains. And in the tropical zone, you can usually expect a forecast of extreme heat and frequent rain. But climate can change over time—especially when it gets help from us.

Most of our energy comes from burning fossil fuels. These fuels contribute to climate change—the slow warming of Earth's temperatures. A few degrees may be hard for us to feel, but warming has a big impact on the global environment. Check out just a handful of global warming's effects on an Arctic habitat.

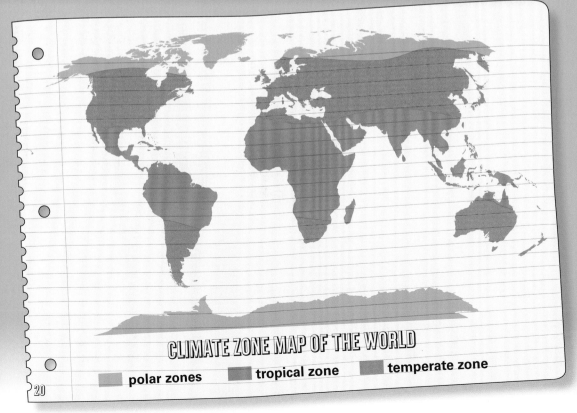

CLIMATE ZONE MAP OF THE WORLD

polar zones   tropical zone   temperate zone

SEA ICE MELTS DUE TO RISING TEMPERATURES

Polar bears cannot travel on sea ice to hunt seals. Instead, they must swim long distances to find food.

Harp seals have less sea ice to use as breeding grounds.

Swimming uses more energy than walking on ice. Polar bears need more food to give them the energy to survive.

More newborn seals die in the harsh conditions. The harp seal population drops. Fewer seals are available for polar bears to eat.

Polar bear populations drop.

Unlike ice, which reflects heat, dark water absorbs heat, helping temperatures rise.

When ice melts, it becomes dark ocean water.

TROPICAL RAIN FORESTS

Lush, vibrant, and teeming with life, rain forests are vital to Earth's health. These huge forests are usually found along the equator, in the tropical climate zone. Temperatures are hot. In most cases, rain falls nearly all year long.

A rain forest is a complex, unique habitat made up of different layers. Each layer plays a role in the forest's cycles. Life thrives in these unique habitats, and it affects the entire world. Here's what rain forests do for Earth:

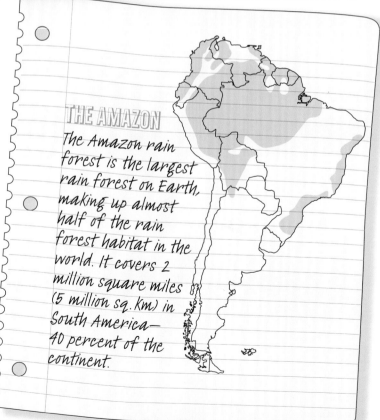

THE AMAZON

The Amazon rain forest is the largest rain forest on Earth, making up almost half of the rain forest habitat in the world. It covers 2 million square miles (5 million sq. km) in South America—40 percent of the continent.

EMERGENTS

150 feet (46 m)

CANOPY

65 feet (20 m)

UNDERSTORY

30 feet (9 m)

SHRUB LAYER

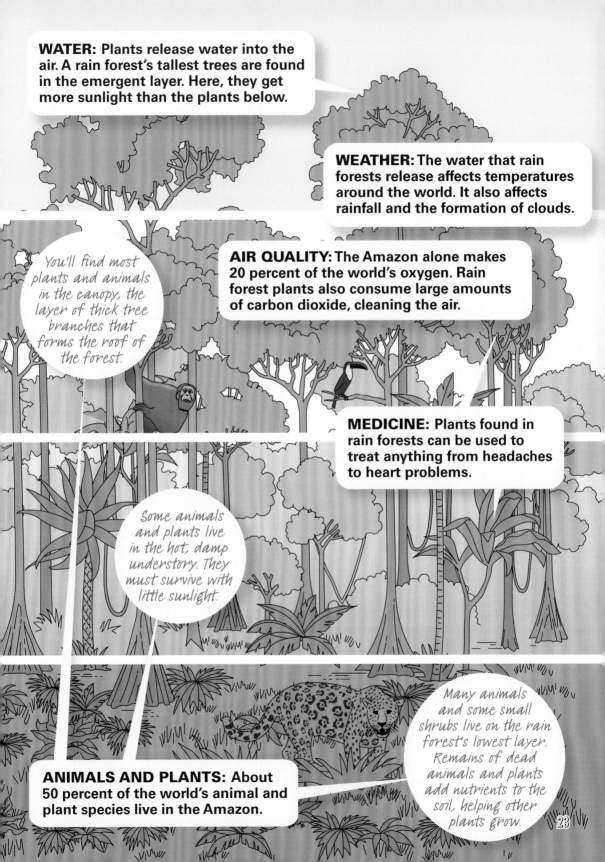

WATER: Plants release water into the air. A rain forest's tallest trees are found in the emergent layer. Here, they get more sunlight than the plants below.

WEATHER: The water that rain forests release affects temperatures around the world. It also affects rainfall and the formation of clouds.

You'll find most plants and animals in the canopy, the layer of thick tree branches that forms the roof of the forest.

AIR QUALITY: The Amazon alone makes 20 percent of the world's oxygen. Rain forest plants also consume large amounts of carbon dioxide, cleaning the air.

MEDICINE: Plants found in rain forests can be used to treat anything from headaches to heart problems.

Some animals and plants live in the hot, damp understory. They must survive with little sunlight.

ANIMALS AND PLANTS: About 50 percent of the world's animal and plant species live in the Amazon.

Many animals and some small shrubs live on the rain forest's lowest layer. Remains of dead animals and plants add nutrients to the soil, helping other plants grow.

AT THE EPICENTER

The ground seems pretty solid, right? Mostly it is, but it is not sitting still. Beneath your feet, huge slabs of rock are slowly, constantly moving on Earth's crust. These plates cover the entire Earth. Their edges rub against one another as they move. When a plate cracks or slips, energy is released as an earthquake. An earthquake starts at a central point where the plates meet—the epicenter—and energy radiates out from that point. Big earthquakes, like many natural disasters, can cause major destruction. Take a look at the biggest one on record—the 1960 earthquake in Chile.

AUSTRALIA

NEW ZEALAND

WAVE HEIGHTS
Up to 80 feet (25 m)

TSUNAMI WAVES
Massive waves radiate across the Pacific Ocean, traveling nearly halfway around the world. Most of this earthquake's damage is caused by tsunami waves. The hardest-hit places are Chile, Japan, and Hawaii. But waves also hit the US west coast, Australia, the Philippines, and New Zealand.

GROUND SHAKING
Buildings crumble. Nearly 60,000 homes are completely destroyed.

FLOODING
Floods destroy trees and move houses up to 2 miles (3 km).

EPICENTER

The epicenter was located on the seafloor.

Nazca Plate

South American Plate

CHILE

MAGNITUDE: 9.5

PLATE BOUNDARY - - - -

DEATH TOLL
Approximately 1,600 people died and 3,000 were injured in Chile.

0   1,000 Miles

SMOG ATTACK

Natural disasters aren't the only dangers our planet faces. Human activity can change the very face of the globe—and not just in remote regions such as the Arctic and tropical rain forests. Every day, the effects of human processes slowly transform the geography of some of the world's busiest cities. Exhibit A: smog.

Smog is fog mixed with smoke. It's a type of air pollution that forms visible clouds. Remember those fossil fuels? They're the main cause of smog. You'll usually find smog in cities where lots of cars and large numbers of factories burn fossil fuels. See how the spread of smog affects a city's landscape.

Sunlight hits air filled with this pollution. This causes the air to turn brown or gray, creating a smog fog. It becomes hard to see through the thick, dark fog.

Cars and factories emit carbon dioxide and other harmful particles into the air.

THE GREAT SMOG

In 1952, London experienced one of the worst smog outbreaks in history. For four days, the fog was so thick that the whole city shut down. About 4,000 people died from breathing in the polluted air. After the tragedy, the United Kingdom passed laws to reduce pollution. But particulate matter—tiny, toxic particles in the air—is still a major problem in cities around the world.

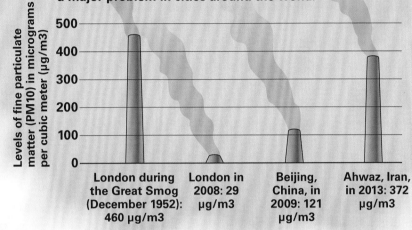

Air pollution can create acid rain. This toxic water falls back to Earth and goes into lakes, rivers, and oceans. It hurts the soil. It also causes buildings to decay.

People breathe in the smog. It causes health problems in the heart and the lungs, including cancer and asthma. Smog can also irritate the eyes.

Plants breathe in carbon dioxide through pores on their leaves and release oxygen. But too much carbon dioxide clogs up plants' pores and stops them from breathing.

TRAPPED IN ICE

With Earth's geography changing all the time, how can we keep track of it? And how can we even begin to guess what our planet used to be like? Many secrets of our geographical past lie hidden in Earth itself.

Ice can be ancient. In the coldest parts of the world, some ice has been around for millions of years. This old ice is found in ice sheets, which cover Antarctica and most of Greenland. In these places, ice is a bit like a time capsule. Every year it traps climate clues in its layers— bits of dust, gases, and water molecules.

Ice cores are long cylinders of ice that have many layers. Looking at the layers tells you how the climate has changed over thousands of years. Go back in time with a look at the layers of an ice core.

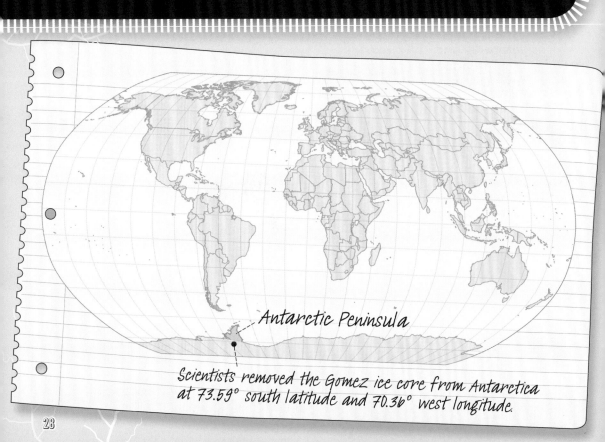

Antarctic Peninsula

Scientists removed the Gomez ice core from Antarctica at 73.59° south latitude and 70.36° west longitude.

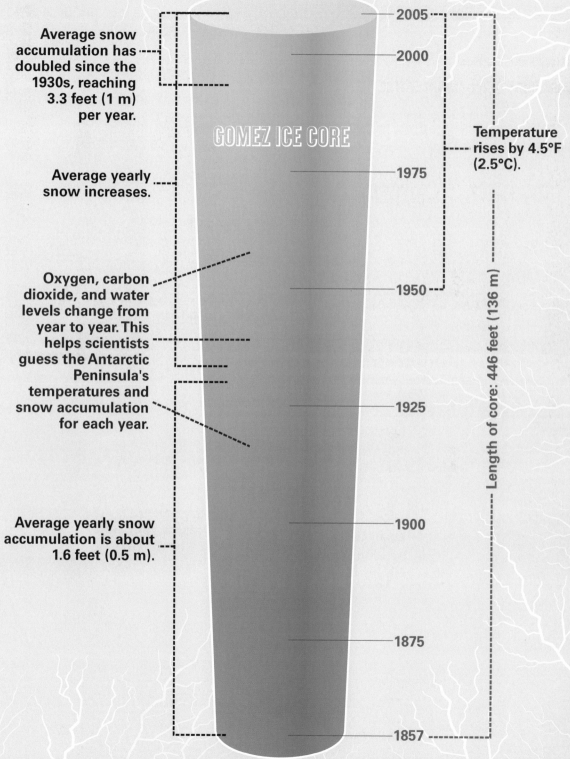

GOMEZ ICE CORE

Average snow accumulation has doubled since the 1930s, reaching 3.3 feet (1 m) per year.

Average yearly snow increases.

Oxygen, carbon dioxide, and water levels change from year to year. This helps scientists guess the Antarctic Peninsula's temperatures and snow accumulation for each year.

Average yearly snow accumulation is about 1.6 feet (0.5 m).

Temperature rises by 4.5°F (2.5°C).

Length of core: 446 feet (136 m)

2005
2000
1975
1950
1925
1900
1875
1857

Glossary

CARBON DIOXIDE: a gas that contains oxygen and carbon, breathed out by people and breathed in by plants

CLIMATE: the set of conditions, including temperature, precipitation, and wind, that are common in a region

CLIMATE ZONE: a large area of the planet based on its latitude and overall climate

CONTINENT: one of the seven large masses of land on Earth—North America, South America, Antarctica, Africa, Asia, Europe, and Australia

HABITAT: the natural place where plants and animals live

LATITUDE: the position of a place measured in degrees, showing the distance north or south of the equator

LONGITUDE: the position of a place measured in degrees, showing the distance east or west of an imaginary line running from pole to pole on Earth

MARITIME: related to the sea

MOLECULE: the smallest part of a substance

POLE: one of the two geographical points on Earth that is farthest away from the equator

RELIEF: the height of a landform compared to the height of the surrounding land or water

SEA LEVEL: the average level of the ocean's surface, which is used to measure the height or depth of places

TURBINE: a large engine powered by spinning blades, which are moved by gas, steam, water, or wind

Further Information

Fridell, Ron. *Earth-Friendly Energy.* Minneapolis: Lerner Publications, 2009. Discover how using fossil fuels harms Earth and which other energy sources do not harm our planet.

Higgins, Nadia. *Natural Disasters through Infographics.* Minneapolis: Lerner Publications, 2014. See the facts about how much damage natural disasters cause on Earth.

Knauer, Kelly. *TIME Living Wonders: The Marvels and Mysteries of Life on Earth.* Minneapolis: Twenty-First Century Books, 2009. Learn about the mysteries of the planet in this book.

NASA Climate Kids: "Huge Machine Harnesses the Tides" http://climatekids.nasa.gov /tidal-energy
Read this article to learn about tidal turbines and the ocean's power.

National Geographic Kids: "Polar Bears Listed as Threatened" http://kids.nationalgeographic .com/kids/stories/animalsnature /polar-bears-threatened
Find out about climate change's effects on polar bears and their Arctic habitat.

National Geographic Society. *National Geographic Kids World Atlas.* Washington, DC: National Geographic Children's Books, 2013. Find amazing maps of places around the world, along with interesting facts.

Storad, Conrad J. *Uncovering Earth's Crust.* Minneapolis: Lerner Publications, 2013. Read about the growing and changing outer layer of Earth.

Index